# CHURCH
# MEMBERSHIP
# RECORD BOOK

# Table of Contents

# MEMBERSHIP SUMMARY

## Membership Summary

| Date | Number(s) of Old Members | Number(s) of New Members Added | Member(s) that have left | Total Number of members |
|---|---|---|---|---|
| | | | | |
| | | | | |
| | | | | |
| | | | | |
| | | | | |
| | | | | |
| | | | | |
| | | | | |
| | | | | |
| | | | | |
| | | | | |
| | | | | |
| | | | | |
| | | | | |
| | | | | |
| | | | | |
| | | | | |
| | | | | |
| | | | | |
| | | | | |
| | | | | |
| | | | | |
| | | | | |

# Membership Summary

| Date | Number(s) of Old Members | Number(s) of New Members Added | Member(s) that have left | Total Number of members |
|------|--------------------------|--------------------------------|--------------------------|-------------------------|
|      |                          |                                |                          |                         |
|      |                          |                                |                          |                         |
|      |                          |                                |                          |                         |
|      |                          |                                |                          |                         |
|      |                          |                                |                          |                         |
|      |                          |                                |                          |                         |
|      |                          |                                |                          |                         |
|      |                          |                                |                          |                         |
|      |                          |                                |                          |                         |
|      |                          |                                |                          |                         |
|      |                          |                                |                          |                         |
|      |                          |                                |                          |                         |
|      |                          |                                |                          |                         |
|      |                          |                                |                          |                         |
|      |                          |                                |                          |                         |
|      |                          |                                |                          |                         |
|      |                          |                                |                          |                         |
|      |                          |                                |                          |                         |
|      |                          |                                |                          |                         |
|      |                          |                                |                          |                         |
|      |                          |                                |                          |                         |
|      |                          |                                |                          |                         |
|      |                          |                                |                          |                         |
|      |                          |                                |                          |                         |
|      |                          |                                |                          |                         |
|      |                          |                                |                          |                         |
|      |                          |                                |                          |                         |

## Membership Summary

| Date | Number(s) of Old Members | Number(s) of New Members Added | Member(s) that have left | Total Number of members |
|------|--------------------------|-------------------------------|--------------------------|-------------------------|
|      |                          |                               |                          |                         |
|      |                          |                               |                          |                         |
|      |                          |                               |                          |                         |
|      |                          |                               |                          |                         |
|      |                          |                               |                          |                         |
|      |                          |                               |                          |                         |
|      |                          |                               |                          |                         |
|      |                          |                               |                          |                         |
|      |                          |                               |                          |                         |
|      |                          |                               |                          |                         |
|      |                          |                               |                          |                         |
|      |                          |                               |                          |                         |
|      |                          |                               |                          |                         |
|      |                          |                               |                          |                         |
|      |                          |                               |                          |                         |
|      |                          |                               |                          |                         |
|      |                          |                               |                          |                         |
|      |                          |                               |                          |                         |
|      |                          |                               |                          |                         |
|      |                          |                               |                          |                         |
|      |                          |                               |                          |                         |
|      |                          |                               |                          |                         |
|      |                          |                               |                          |                         |
|      |                          |                               |                          |                         |
|      |                          |                               |                          |                         |

Membership Summary

# Membership Summary

| Date | Number(s) of Old Members | Number(s) of New Members Added | Member(s) that have left | Total Number of members |
|------|--------------------------|--------------------------------|--------------------------|-------------------------|
|      |                          |                                |                          |                         |
|      |                          |                                |                          |                         |
|      |                          |                                |                          |                         |
|      |                          |                                |                          |                         |
|      |                          |                                |                          |                         |
|      |                          |                                |                          |                         |
|      |                          |                                |                          |                         |
|      |                          |                                |                          |                         |
|      |                          |                                |                          |                         |
|      |                          |                                |                          |                         |
|      |                          |                                |                          |                         |
|      |                          |                                |                          |                         |
|      |                          |                                |                          |                         |
|      |                          |                                |                          |                         |
|      |                          |                                |                          |                         |
|      |                          |                                |                          |                         |
|      |                          |                                |                          |                         |
|      |                          |                                |                          |                         |
|      |                          |                                |                          |                         |
|      |                          |                                |                          |                         |
|      |                          |                                |                          |                         |
|      |                          |                                |                          |                         |
|      |                          |                                |                          |                         |
|      |                          |                                |                          |                         |
|      |                          |                                |                          |                         |
|      |                          |                                |                          |                         |

# APPOINTMENT LOG

Appointment Log

| Serial No. | Name | Visiting Date | No of People Visited | Remarks |
|---|---|---|---|---|
| | | | | |
| | | | | |
| | | | | |
| | | | | |
| | | | | |
| | | | | |
| | | | | |
| | | | | |
| | | | | |
| | | | | |
| | | | | |
| | | | | |
| | | | | |
| | | | | |
| | | | | |
| | | | | |
| | | | | |
| | | | | |
| | | | | |
| | | | | |
| | | | | |
| | | | | |
| | | | | |
| | | | | |
| | | | | |

# Appointment Log

| Serial No. | Name | Visiting Date | No of People Visited | Remarks |
|---|---|---|---|---|
| | | | | |
| | | | | |
| | | | | |
| | | | | |
| | | | | |
| | | | | |
| | | | | |
| | | | | |
| | | | | |
| | | | | |
| | | | | |
| | | | | |
| | | | | |
| | | | | |
| | | | | |
| | | | | |
| | | | | |
| | | | | |
| | | | | |
| | | | | |
| | | | | |
| | | | | |
| | | | | |
| | | | | |
| | | | | |

## Appointment Log

| Serial No. | Name | Visiting Date | No of People Visited | Remarks |
|---|---|---|---|---|
| | | | | |
| | | | | |
| | | | | |
| | | | | |
| | | | | |
| | | | | |
| | | | | |
| | | | | |
| | | | | |
| | | | | |
| | | | | |
| | | | | |
| | | | | |
| | | | | |
| | | | | |
| | | | | |
| | | | | |
| | | | | |
| | | | | |
| | | | | |
| | | | | |
| | | | | |
| | | | | |

# Appointment Log

| Serial No. | Name | Visiting Date | No of People Visited | Remarks |
|---|---|---|---|---|
|  |  |  |  |  |
|  |  |  |  |  |
|  |  |  |  |  |
|  |  |  |  |  |
|  |  |  |  |  |
|  |  |  |  |  |
|  |  |  |  |  |
|  |  |  |  |  |
|  |  |  |  |  |
|  |  |  |  |  |
|  |  |  |  |  |
|  |  |  |  |  |
|  |  |  |  |  |
|  |  |  |  |  |
|  |  |  |  |  |
|  |  |  |  |  |
|  |  |  |  |  |
|  |  |  |  |  |
|  |  |  |  |  |
|  |  |  |  |  |
|  |  |  |  |  |
|  |  |  |  |  |
|  |  |  |  |  |
|  |  |  |  |  |

# ALPHABETICAL MEMBERSHIP RECORD

# A

| Name | |
|---|---|
| Address | |
| | |

| Phone Numbers | Mobile: | Home: |
|---|---|---|
| Email | | |
| Birthday | | Membership date: |
| Gender | | |
| Marital Status | | Wedding Anniversary: |

| Name | |
|---|---|
| Address | |
| | |

| Phone Numbers | Mobile: | Home: |
|---|---|---|
| Email | | |
| Birthday | | Membership date: |
| Gender | | |
| Marital Status | | Wedding Anniversary: |

| Name | |
|---|---|
| Address | |
| | |

| Phone Numbers | Mobile: | Home: |
|---|---|---|
| Email | | |
| Birthday | | Membership date: |
| Gender | | |
| Marital Status | | Wedding Anniversary: |

# A

| Name | |
|---|---|
| Address | |
| | |

| Phone Numbers | Mobile: | Home: |
|---|---|---|

| Email | |
|---|---|

| Birthday | | Membership date: |
|---|---|---|

| Gender | |
|---|---|

| Marital Status | | Wedding Anniversary: |
|---|---|---|

| Name | |
|---|---|
| Address | |
| | |

| Phone Numbers | Mobile: | Home: |
|---|---|---|

| Email | |
|---|---|

| Birthday | | Membership date: |
|---|---|---|

| Gender | |
|---|---|

| Marital Status | | Wedding Anniversary: |
|---|---|---|

| Name | |
|---|---|
| Address | |
| | |

| Phone Numbers | Mobile: | Home: |
|---|---|---|

| Email | |
|---|---|

| Birthday | | Membership date: |
|---|---|---|

| Gender | |
|---|---|

| Marital Status | | Wedding Anniversary: |
|---|---|---|

## A

| Name | |
|---|---|
| Address | |
| | |

| Phone Numbers | Mobile: | Home: |
|---|---|---|
| Email | | |
| Birthday | Membership date: | |
| Gender | | |
| Marital Status | Wedding Anniversary: | |

| Name | |
|---|---|
| Address | |
| | |

| Phone Numbers | Mobile: | Home: |
|---|---|---|
| Email | | |
| Birthday | Membership date: | |
| Gender | | |
| Marital Status | Wedding Anniversary: | |

| Name | |
|---|---|
| Address | |
| | |

| Phone Numbers | Mobile: | Home: |
|---|---|---|
| Email | | |
| Birthday | Membership date: | |
| Gender | | |
| Marital Status | Wedding Anniversary: | |

# A

| Name | |
|---|---|
| **Address** | |
| | |
| **Phone Numbers** | **Mobile:** **Home:** |
| **Email** | |
| **Birthday** | **Membership date:** |
| **Gender** | |
| **Marital Status** | **Wedding Anniversary:** |

| Name | |
|---|---|
| **Address** | |
| | |
| **Phone Numbers** | **Mobile:** **Home:** |
| **Email** | |
| **Birthday** | **Membership date:** |
| **Gender** | |
| **Marital Status** | **Wedding Anniversary:** |

| Name | |
|---|---|
| **Address** | |
| | |
| **Phone Numbers** | **Mobile:** **Home:** |
| **Email** | |
| **Birthday** | **Membership date:** |
| **Gender** | |
| **Marital Status** | **Wedding Anniversary:** |

# B

| | | |
|---|---|---|
| **Name** | | |
| **Address** | | |
| | | |
| **Phone Numbers** | **Mobile:** | **Home:** |
| **Email** | | |
| **Birthday** | | **Membership date:** |
| **Gender** | | |
| **Marital Status** | | **Wedding Anniversary:** |

| | | |
|---|---|---|
| **Name** | | |
| **Address** | | |
| | | |
| **Phone Numbers** | **Mobile:** | **Home:** |
| **Email** | | |
| **Birthday** | | **Membership date:** |
| **Gender** | | |
| **Marital Status** | | **Wedding Anniversary:** |

| | | |
|---|---|---|
| **Name** | | |
| **Address** | | |
| | | |
| **Phone Numbers** | **Mobile:** | **Home:** |
| **Email** | | |
| **Birthday** | | **Membership date:** |
| **Gender** | | |
| **Marital Status** | | **Wedding Anniversary:** |

# B

| Name | |
|---|---|
| Address | |
| | |
| **Phone Numbers** | Mobile:        Home: |
| Email | |
| Birthday | Membership date: |
| Gender | |
| Marital Status | Wedding Anniversary: |

| Name | |
|---|---|
| Address | |
| | |
| **Phone Numbers** | Mobile:        Home: |
| Email | |
| Birthday | Membership date: |
| Gender | |
| Marital Status | Wedding Anniversary: |

| Name | |
|---|---|
| Address | |
| | |
| **Phone Numbers** | Mobile:        Home: |
| Email | |
| Birthday | Membership date: |
| Gender | |
| Marital Status | Wedding Anniversary: |

# B

| Name | |
|---|---|
| Address | |
| | |

| Phone Numbers | Mobile: | Home: |
|---|---|---|

| Email | |
|---|---|

| Birthday | | Membership date: |
|---|---|---|

| Gender | |
|---|---|

| Marital Status | | Wedding Anniversary: |
|---|---|---|

| Name | |
|---|---|
| Address | |
| | |

| Phone Numbers | Mobile: | Home: |
|---|---|---|

| Email | |
|---|---|

| Birthday | | Membership date: |
|---|---|---|

| Gender | |
|---|---|

| Marital Status | | Wedding Anniversary: |
|---|---|---|

| Name | |
|---|---|
| Address | |
| | |

| Phone Numbers | Mobile: | Home: |
|---|---|---|

| Email | |
|---|---|

| Birthday | | Membership date: |
|---|---|---|

| Gender | |
|---|---|

| Marital Status | | Wedding Anniversary: |
|---|---|---|

## B

| Name | |
|---|---|
| **Address** | |
| | |
| **Phone Numbers** | **Mobile:** — **Home:** |
| **Email** | |
| **Birthday** | **Membership date:** |
| **Gender** | |
| **Marital Status** | **Wedding Anniversary:** |

| Name | |
|---|---|
| **Address** | |
| | |
| **Phone Numbers** | **Mobile:** — **Home:** |
| **Email** | |
| **Birthday** | **Membership date:** |
| **Gender** | |
| **Marital Status** | **Wedding Anniversary:** |

| Name | |
|---|---|
| **Address** | |
| | |
| **Phone Numbers** | **Mobile:** — **Home:** |
| **Email** | |
| **Birthday** | **Membership date:** |
| **Gender** | |
| **Marital Status** | **Wedding Anniversary:** |

# C

| Name | |
|---|---|
| Address | |
| | |
| Phone Numbers | Mobile:        Home: |
| Email | |
| Birthday | Membership date: |
| Gender | |
| Marital Status | Wedding Anniversary: |

| Name | |
|---|---|
| Address | |
| | |
| Phone Numbers | Mobile:        Home: |
| Email | |
| Birthday | Membership date: |
| Gender | |
| Marital Status | Wedding Anniversary: |

| Name | |
|---|---|
| Address | |
| | |
| Phone Numbers | Mobile:        Home: |
| Email | |
| Birthday | Membership date: |
| Gender | |
| Marital Status | Wedding Anniversary: |

## C

| Name | |
|---|---|
| Address | |
| | |

| Phone Numbers | Mobile: | Home: |
|---|---|---|
| Email | | |
| Birthday | | Membership date: |
| Gender | | |
| Marital Status | | Wedding Anniversary: |

| Name | |
|---|---|
| Address | |
| | |

| Phone Numbers | Mobile: | Home: |
|---|---|---|
| Email | | |
| Birthday | | Membership date: |
| Gender | | |
| Marital Status | | Wedding Anniversary: |

| Name | |
|---|---|
| Address | |
| | |

| Phone Numbers | Mobile: | Home: |
|---|---|---|
| Email | | |
| Birthday | | Membership date: |
| Gender | | |
| Marital Status | | Wedding Anniversary: |

## C

| Name | |
|---|---|
| Address | |
| | |

| Phone Numbers | Mobile: | Home: |
|---|---|---|
| Email | | |
| Birthday | | Membership date: |
| Gender | | |
| Marital Status | | Wedding Anniversary: |

| Name | |
|---|---|
| Address | |
| | |

| Phone Numbers | Mobile: | Home: |
|---|---|---|
| Email | | |
| Birthday | | Membership date: |
| Gender | | |
| Marital Status | | Wedding Anniversary: |

| Name | |
|---|---|
| Address | |
| | |

| Phone Numbers | Mobile: | Home: |
|---|---|---|
| Email | | |
| Birthday | | Membership date: |
| Gender | | |
| Marital Status | | Wedding Anniversary: |

# C

| Name | |
|---|---|
| Address | |
| | |

| Phone Numbers | Mobile: | Home: |
|---|---|---|
| Email | | |
| Birthday | | Membership date: |
| Gender | | |

| Marital Status | | Wedding Anniversary: |
|---|---|---|

| Name | |
|---|---|
| Address | |
| | |

| Phone Numbers | Mobile: | Home: |
|---|---|---|
| Email | | |
| Birthday | | Membership date: |
| Gender | | |

| Marital Status | | Wedding Anniversary: |
|---|---|---|

| Name | |
|---|---|
| Address | |
| | |

| Phone Numbers | Mobile: | Home: |
|---|---|---|
| Email | | |
| Birthday | | Membership date: |
| Gender | | |

| Marital Status | | Wedding Anniversary: |
|---|---|---|

# D

| Name | |
|---|---|
| Address | |
| | |
| Phone Numbers | Mobile: Home: |
| Email | |
| Birthday | Membership date: |
| Gender | |
| Marital Status | Wedding Anniversary: |

| Name | |
|---|---|
| Address | |
| | |
| Phone Numbers | Mobile: Home: |
| Email | |
| Birthday | Membership date: |
| Gender | |
| Marital Status | Wedding Anniversary: |

| Name | |
|---|---|
| Address | |
| | |
| Phone Numbers | Mobile: Home: |
| Email | |
| Birthday | Membership date: |
| Gender | |
| Marital Status | Wedding Anniversary: |

# D

| Name | |
|---|---|
| Address | |
| | |

| Phone Numbers | Mobile: | Home: |
|---|---|---|
| Email | | |
| Birthday | | Membership date: |
| Gender | | |
| Marital Status | | Wedding Anniversary: |

| Name | |
|---|---|
| Address | |
| | |

| Phone Numbers | Mobile: | Home: |
|---|---|---|
| Email | | |
| Birthday | | Membership date: |
| Gender | | |
| Marital Status | | Wedding Anniversary: |

| Name | |
|---|---|
| Address | |
| | |

| Phone Numbers | Mobile: | Home: |
|---|---|---|
| Email | | |
| Birthday | | Membership date: |
| Gender | | |
| Marital Status | | Wedding Anniversary: |

# D

| Name | |
|---|---|
| Address | |
| | |
| Phone Numbers | Mobile: Home: |
| Email | |
| Birthday | Membership date: |
| Gender | |
| Marital Status | Wedding Anniversary: |

| Name | |
|---|---|
| Address | |
| | |
| Phone Numbers | Mobile: Home: |
| Email | |
| Birthday | Membership date: |
| Gender | |
| Marital Status | Wedding Anniversary: |

| Name | |
|---|---|
| Address | |
| | |
| Phone Numbers | Mobile: Home: |
| Email | |
| Birthday | Membership date: |
| Gender | |
| Marital Status | Wedding Anniversary: |

# D

| Name | |
|---|---|
| Address | |
| | |

| Phone Numbers | Mobile: | Home: |
|---|---|---|

| Email | |
|---|---|

| Birthday | Membership date: |
|---|---|

| Gender | |
|---|---|

| Marital Status | Wedding Anniversary: |
|---|---|

| Name | |
|---|---|
| Address | |
| | |

| Phone Numbers | Mobile: | Home: |
|---|---|---|

| Email | |
|---|---|

| Birthday | Membership date: |
|---|---|

| Gender | |
|---|---|

| Marital Status | Wedding Anniversary: |
|---|---|

| Name | |
|---|---|
| Address | |
| | |

| Phone Numbers | Mobile: | Home: |
|---|---|---|

| Email | |
|---|---|

| Birthday | Membership date: |
|---|---|

| Gender | |
|---|---|

| Marital Status | Wedding Anniversary: |
|---|---|

# E

| Name | |
|---|---|
| Address | |
| | |

| Phone Numbers | Mobile: | Home: |
|---|---|---|
| Email | | |
| Birthday | | Membership date: |
| Gender | | |
| Marital Status | | Wedding Anniversary: |

| Name | |
|---|---|
| Address | |
| | |

| Phone Numbers | Mobile: | Home: |
|---|---|---|
| Email | | |
| Birthday | | Membership date: |
| Gender | | |
| Marital Status | | Wedding Anniversary: |

| Name | |
|---|---|
| Address | |
| | |

| Phone Numbers | Mobile: | Home: |
|---|---|---|
| Email | | |
| Birthday | | Membership date: |
| Gender | | |
| Marital Status | | Wedding Anniversary: |

# E

| Name | |
|---|---|
| Address | |
| | |

| Phone Numbers | Mobile: | Home: |
|---|---|---|
| Email | | |
| Birthday | | Membership date: |
| Gender | | |
| Marital Status | | Wedding Anniversary: |

| Name | |
|---|---|
| Address | |
| | |

| Phone Numbers | Mobile: | Home: |
|---|---|---|
| Email | | |
| Birthday | | Membership date: |
| Gender | | |
| Marital Status | | Wedding Anniversary: |

| Name | |
|---|---|
| Address | |
| | |

| Phone Numbers | Mobile: | Home: |
|---|---|---|
| Email | | |
| Birthday | | Membership date: |
| Gender | | |
| Marital Status | | Wedding Anniversary: |

# E

| Name | |
|---|---|
| Address | |
| | |
| Phone Numbers | Mobile: | Home: |
| Email | |
| Birthday | Membership date: |
| Gender | |
| Marital Status | Wedding Anniversary: |

| Name | |
|---|---|
| Address | |
| | |
| Phone Numbers | Mobile: | Home: |
| Email | |
| Birthday | Membership date: |
| Gender | |
| Marital Status | Wedding Anniversary: |

| Name | |
|---|---|
| Address | |
| | |
| Phone Numbers | Mobile: | Home: |
| Email | |
| Birthday | Membership date: |
| Gender | |
| Marital Status | Wedding Anniversary: |

## E

| Name | |
|---|---|
| Address | |
| | |
| Phone Numbers | Mobile:      Home: |
| Email | |
| Birthday |      Membership date: |
| Gender | |
| Marital Status |      Wedding Anniversary: |

| Name | |
|---|---|
| Address | |
| | |
| Phone Numbers | Mobile:      Home: |
| Email | |
| Birthday |      Membership date: |
| Gender | |
| Marital Status |      Wedding Anniversary: |

| Name | |
|---|---|
| Address | |
| | |
| Phone Numbers | Mobile:      Home: |
| Email | |
| Birthday |      Membership date: |
| Gender | |
| Marital Status |      Wedding Anniversary: |

## F

| Name | |
|---|---|
| Address | |
| | |
| Phone Numbers | Mobile: | Home: |
| Email | |
| Birthday | Membership date: |
| Gender | |
| Marital Status | Wedding Anniversary: |

| Name | |
|---|---|
| Address | |
| | |
| Phone Numbers | Mobile: | Home: |
| Email | |
| Birthday | Membership date: |
| Gender | |
| Marital Status | Wedding Anniversary: |

| Name | |
|---|---|
| Address | |
| | |
| Phone Numbers | Mobile: | Home: |
| Email | |
| Birthday | Membership date: |
| Gender | |
| Marital Status | Wedding Anniversary: |

## F

| Name | |
|---|---|
| Address | |
| | |

| Phone Numbers | Mobile: | Home: |
|---|---|---|
| Email | | |
| Birthday | | Membership date: |
| Gender | | |
| Marital Status | | Wedding Anniversary: |

| Name | |
|---|---|
| Address | |
| | |

| Phone Numbers | Mobile: | Home: |
|---|---|---|
| Email | | |
| Birthday | | Membership date: |
| Gender | | |
| Marital Status | | Wedding Anniversary: |

| Name | |
|---|---|
| Address | |
| | |

| Phone Numbers | Mobile: | Home: |
|---|---|---|
| Email | | |
| Birthday | | Membership date: |
| Gender | | |
| Marital Status | | Wedding Anniversary: |

## F

| Name | |
|---|---|
| Address | |
| | |
| **Phone Numbers** Mobile: | Home: |
| Email | |
| Birthday | Membership date: |
| Gender | |
| Marital Status | Wedding Anniversary: |

| Name | |
|---|---|
| Address | |
| | |
| **Phone Numbers** Mobile: | Home: |
| Email | |
| Birthday | Membership date: |
| Gender | |
| Marital Status | Wedding Anniversary: |

| Name | |
|---|---|
| Address | |
| | |
| **Phone Numbers** Mobile: | Home: |
| Email | |
| Birthday | Membership date: |
| Gender | |
| Marital Status | Wedding Anniversary: |

# F

| Name | |
|---|---|
| Address | |
| | |
| Phone Numbers | Mobile: |
| Email | |
| Birthday | Membership date: |
| Gender | |
| Marital Status | Wedding Anniversary: |

| Name | |
|---|---|
| Address | |
| | |
| Phone Numbers | Mobile: |
| Email | |
| Birthday | Membership date: |
| Gender | |
| Marital Status | Wedding Anniversary: |

| Name | |
|---|---|
| Address | |
| | |
| Phone Numbers | Mobile: |
| Email | |
| Birthday | Membership date: |
| Gender | |
| Marital Status | Wedding Anniversary: |

Home:

Home:

Home:

## G

| Name | |
|---|---|
| Address | |
| | |

| Phone Numbers | Mobile: | Home: |
|---|---|---|
| Email | | |
| Birthday | | Membership date: |
| Gender | | |
| Marital Status | | Wedding Anniversary: |

| Name | |
|---|---|
| Address | |
| | |

| Phone Numbers | Mobile: | Home: |
|---|---|---|
| Email | | |
| Birthday | | Membership date: |
| Gender | | |
| Marital Status | | Wedding Anniversary: |

| Name | |
|---|---|
| Address | |
| | |

| Phone Numbers | Mobile: | Home: |
|---|---|---|
| Email | | |
| Birthday | | Membership date: |
| Gender | | |
| Marital Status | | Wedding Anniversary: |

# G

| Name | |
|---|---|
| Address | |
| | |
| Phone Numbers | Mobile: | Home: |
| Email | |
| Birthday | Membership date: |
| Gender | |
| Marital Status | Wedding Anniversary: |

| Name | |
|---|---|
| Address | |
| | |
| Phone Numbers | Mobile: | Home: |
| Email | |
| Birthday | Membership date: |
| Gender | |
| Marital Status | Wedding Anniversary: |

| Name | |
|---|---|
| Address | |
| | |
| Phone Numbers | Mobile: | Home: |
| Email | |
| Birthday | Membership date: |
| Gender | |
| Marital Status | Wedding Anniversary: |

# G

| Name | |
|---|---|
| Address | |
| | |
| Phone Numbers | Mobile: | Home: |
| Email | |
| Birthday | | Membership date: |
| Gender | |
| Marital Status | | Wedding Anniversary: |

| Name | |
|---|---|
| Address | |
| | |
| Phone Numbers | Mobile: | Home: |
| Email | |
| Birthday | | Membership date: |
| Gender | |
| Marital Status | | Wedding Anniversary: |

| Name | |
|---|---|
| Address | |
| | |
| Phone Numbers | Mobile: | Home: |
| Email | |
| Birthday | | Membership date: |
| Gender | |
| Marital Status | | Wedding Anniversary: |

# G

| Name | |
|---|---|
| Address | |
| | |
| Phone Numbers | Mobile:       Home: |
| Email | |
| Birthday |       Membership date: |
| Gender | |
| Marital Status |       Wedding Anniversary: |

| Name | |
|---|---|
| Address | |
| | |
| Phone Numbers | Mobile:       Home: |
| Email | |
| Birthday |       Membership date: |
| Gender | |
| Marital Status |       Wedding Anniversary: |

| Name | |
|---|---|
| Address | |
| | |
| Phone Numbers | Mobile:       Home: |
| Email | |
| Birthday |       Membership date: |
| Gender | |
| Marital Status |       Wedding Anniversary: |

# H

| Name | |
|---|---|
| Address | |
| | |
| Phone Numbers | Mobile: Home: |
| Email | |
| Birthday | Membership date: |
| Gender | |
| Marital Status | Wedding Anniversary: |

| Name | |
|---|---|
| Address | |
| | |
| Phone Numbers | Mobile: Home: |
| Email | |
| Birthday | Membership date: |
| Gender | |
| Marital Status | Wedding Anniversary: |

| Name | |
|---|---|
| Address | |
| | |
| Phone Numbers | Mobile: Home: |
| Email | |
| Birthday | Membership date: |
| Gender | |
| Marital Status | Wedding Anniversary: |

# H

| Name | |
|---|---|
| Address | |
| | |
| Phone Numbers | Mobile: | Home: |
| Email | |
| Birthday | Membership date: |
| Gender | |
| Marital Status | Wedding Anniversary: |

| Name | |
|---|---|
| Address | |
| | |
| Phone Numbers | Mobile: | Home: |
| Email | |
| Birthday | Membership date: |
| Gender | |
| Marital Status | Wedding Anniversary: |

| Name | |
|---|---|
| Address | |
| | |
| Phone Numbers | Mobile: | Home: |
| Email | |
| Birthday | Membership date: |
| Gender | |
| Marital Status | Wedding Anniversary: |

# H

| Name | |
|---|---|
| Address | |
| | |

| Phone Numbers | Mobile: | Home: |
|---|---|---|

| Email | |
|---|---|

| Birthday | Membership date: |
|---|---|

| Gender | |
|---|---|

| Marital Status | Wedding Anniversary: |
|---|---|

| Name | |
|---|---|
| Address | |
| | |

| Phone Numbers | Mobile: | Home: |
|---|---|---|

| Email | |
|---|---|

| Birthday | Membership date: |
|---|---|

| Gender | |
|---|---|

| Marital Status | Wedding Anniversary: |
|---|---|

| Name | |
|---|---|
| Address | |
| | |

| Phone Numbers | Mobile: | Home: |
|---|---|---|

| Email | |
|---|---|

| Birthday | Membership date: |
|---|---|

| Gender | |
|---|---|

| Marital Status | Wedding Anniversary: |
|---|---|

# H

| Name | |
|---|---|
| Address | |
| | |

| Phone Numbers | Mobile: | Home: |
|---|---|---|
| Email | | |
| Birthday | | Membership date: |
| Gender | | |
| Marital Status | | Wedding Anniversary: |

| Name | |
|---|---|
| Address | |
| | |

| Phone Numbers | Mobile: | Home: |
|---|---|---|
| Email | | |
| Birthday | | Membership date: |
| Gender | | |
| Marital Status | | Wedding Anniversary: |

| Name | |
|---|---|
| Address | |
| | |

| Phone Numbers | Mobile: | Home: |
|---|---|---|
| Email | | |
| Birthday | | Membership date: |
| Gender | | |
| Marital Status | | Wedding Anniversary: |

# I

| Name | |
|---|---|
| Address | |
| | |
| Phone Numbers | Mobile: | Home: |
| Email | |
| Birthday | | Membership date: |
| Gender | |
| Marital Status | | Wedding Anniversary: |

| Name | |
|---|---|
| Address | |
| | |
| Phone Numbers | Mobile: | Home: |
| Email | |
| Birthday | | Membership date: |
| Gender | |
| Marital Status | | Wedding Anniversary: |

| Name | |
|---|---|
| Address | |
| | |
| Phone Numbers | Mobile: | Home: |
| Email | |
| Birthday | | Membership date: |
| Gender | |
| Marital Status | | Wedding Anniversary: |

## I

| Name | |
|---|---|
| Address | |
| | |

| Phone Numbers | Mobile: | Home: |
|---|---|---|

| Email | |
|---|---|

| Birthday | | Membership date: |
|---|---|---|

| Gender | |
|---|---|

| Marital Status | | Wedding Anniversary: |
|---|---|---|

| Name | |
|---|---|
| Address | |
| | |

| Phone Numbers | Mobile: | Home: |
|---|---|---|

| Email | |
|---|---|

| Birthday | | Membership date: |
|---|---|---|

| Gender | |
|---|---|

| Marital Status | | Wedding Anniversary: |
|---|---|---|

| Name | |
|---|---|
| Address | |
| | |

| Phone Numbers | Mobile: | Home: |
|---|---|---|

| Email | |
|---|---|

| Birthday | | Membership date: |
|---|---|---|

| Gender | |
|---|---|

| Marital Status | | Wedding Anniversary: |
|---|---|---|

## I

| Name | |
|---|---|
| Address | |
| | |
| Phone Numbers | Mobile: |  Home: |
| Email | |
| Birthday | Membership date: |
| Gender | |
| Marital Status | Wedding Anniversary: |

| Name | |
|---|---|
| Address | |
| | |
| Phone Numbers | Mobile: |  Home: |
| Email | |
| Birthday | Membership date: |
| Gender | |
| Marital Status | Wedding Anniversary: |

| Name | |
|---|---|
| Address | |
| | |
| Phone Numbers | Mobile: |  Home: |
| Email | |
| Birthday | Membership date: |
| Gender | |
| Marital Status | Wedding Anniversary: |

| I | |
|---|---|
| **Name** | |
| **Address** | |
| | |
| **Phone Numbers** | **Mobile:**      **Home:** |
| **Email** | |
| **Birthday** | **Membership date:** |
| **Gender** | |
| **Marital Status** | **Wedding Anniversary:** |

| | |
|---|---|
| **Name** | |
| **Address** | |
| | |
| **Phone Numbers** | **Mobile:**      **Home:** |
| **Email** | |
| **Birthday** | **Membership date:** |
| **Gender** | |
| **Marital Status** | **Wedding Anniversary:** |

| | |
|---|---|
| **Name** | |
| **Address** | |
| | |
| **Phone Numbers** | **Mobile:**      **Home:** |
| **Email** | |
| **Birthday** | **Membership date:** |
| **Gender** | |
| **Marital Status** | **Wedding Anniversary:** |

## J

| Name | |
|---|---|
| Address | |
| | |
| Phone Numbers | Mobile: | Home: |
| Email | |
| Birthday | | Membership date: |
| Gender | |
| Marital Status | | Wedding Anniversary: |

| Name | |
|---|---|
| Address | |
| | |
| Phone Numbers | Mobile: | Home: |
| Email | |
| Birthday | | Membership date: |
| Gender | |
| Marital Status | | Wedding Anniversary: |

| Name | |
|---|---|
| Address | |
| | |
| Phone Numbers | Mobile: | Home: |
| Email | |
| Birthday | | Membership date: |
| Gender | |
| Marital Status | | Wedding Anniversary: |

## J

| Name | |
|---|---|
| Address | |
| | |
| Phone Numbers | Mobile: | Home: |
| Email | |
| Birthday | Membership date: |
| Gender | |
| Marital Status | Wedding Anniversary: |

| Name | |
|---|---|
| Address | |
| | |
| Phone Numbers | Mobile: | Home: |
| Email | |
| Birthday | Membership date: |
| Gender | |
| Marital Status | Wedding Anniversary: |

| Name | |
|---|---|
| Address | |
| | |
| Phone Numbers | Mobile: | Home: |
| Email | |
| Birthday | Membership date: |
| Gender | |
| Marital Status | Wedding Anniversary: |

## J

| Name | |
|---|---|
| Address | |
| | |
| Phone Numbers | Mobile: | Home: |
| Email | |
| Birthday | Membership date: |
| Gender | |
| Marital Status | Wedding Anniversary: |

| Name | |
|---|---|
| Address | |
| | |
| Phone Numbers | Mobile: | Home: |
| Email | |
| Birthday | Membership date: |
| Gender | |
| Marital Status | Wedding Anniversary: |

| Name | |
|---|---|
| Address | |
| | |
| Phone Numbers | Mobile: | Home: |
| Email | |
| Birthday | Membership date: |
| Gender | |
| Marital Status | Wedding Anniversary: |

## J

| Name | |
|---|---|
| Address | |
| | |
| Phone Numbers | Mobile: | Home: |
| Email | |
| Birthday | Membership date: |
| Gender | |
| Marital Status | Wedding Anniversary: |

| Name | |
|---|---|
| Address | |
| | |
| Phone Numbers | Mobile: | Home: |
| Email | |
| Birthday | Membership date: |
| Gender | |
| Marital Status | Wedding Anniversary: |

| Name | |
|---|---|
| Address | |
| | |
| Phone Numbers | Mobile: | Home: |
| Email | |
| Birthday | Membership date: |
| Gender | |
| Marital Status | Wedding Anniversary: |

# K

| Name | |
|---|---|
| Address | |
| | |
| Phone Numbers | Mobile: | Home: |
| Email | |
| Birthday | Membership date: |
| Gender | |
| Marital Status | Wedding Anniversary: |

| Name | |
|---|---|
| Address | |
| | |
| Phone Numbers | Mobile: | Home: |
| Email | |
| Birthday | Membership date: |
| Gender | |
| Marital Status | Wedding Anniversary: |

| Name | |
|---|---|
| Address | |
| | |
| Phone Numbers | Mobile: | Home: |
| Email | |
| Birthday | Membership date: |
| Gender | |
| Marital Status | Wedding Anniversary: |

## K

| Name | |
|---|---|
| Address | |
| | |
| **Phone Numbers** | Mobile:       Home: |
| Email | |
| Birthday | Membership date: |
| Gender | |
| Marital Status | Wedding Anniversary: |

| Name | |
|---|---|
| Address | |
| | |
| **Phone Numbers** | Mobile:       Home: |
| Email | |
| Birthday | Membership date: |
| Gender | |
| Marital Status | Wedding Anniversary: |

| Name | |
|---|---|
| Address | |
| | |
| **Phone Numbers** | Mobile:       Home: |
| Email | |
| Birthday | Membership date: |
| Gender | |
| Marital Status | Wedding Anniversary: |

## K

| Name | |
|---|---|
| Address | |
| | |

| Phone Numbers | Mobile: | Home: |
|---|---|---|

| Email | |
|---|---|

| Birthday | | Membership date: |
|---|---|---|

| Gender | |
|---|---|

| Marital Status | | Wedding Anniversary: |
|---|---|---|

| Name | |
|---|---|
| Address | |
| | |

| Phone Numbers | Mobile: | Home: |
|---|---|---|

| Email | |
|---|---|

| Birthday | | Membership date: |
|---|---|---|

| Gender | |
|---|---|

| Marital Status | | Wedding Anniversary: |
|---|---|---|

| Name | |
|---|---|
| Address | |
| | |

| Phone Numbers | Mobile: | Home: |
|---|---|---|

| Email | |
|---|---|

| Birthday | | Membership date: |
|---|---|---|

| Gender | |
|---|---|

| Marital Status | | Wedding Anniversary: |
|---|---|---|

# K

| Name | |
|---|---|
| **Address** | |
| | |
| **Phone Numbers** | **Mobile:** | **Home:** |
| **Email** | |
| **Birthday** | **Membership date:** |
| **Gender** | |
| **Marital Status** | **Wedding Anniversary:** |

| Name | |
|---|---|
| **Address** | |
| | |
| **Phone Numbers** | **Mobile:** | **Home:** |
| **Email** | |
| **Birthday** | **Membership date:** |
| **Gender** | |
| **Marital Status** | **Wedding Anniversary:** |

| Name | |
|---|---|
| **Address** | |
| | |
| **Phone Numbers** | **Mobile:** | **Home:** |
| **Email** | |
| **Birthday** | **Membership date:** |
| **Gender** | |
| **Marital Status** | **Wedding Anniversary:** |

## L

| Name | |
|---|---|
| Address | |
| | |

| Phone Numbers | Mobile: | Home: |
|---|---|---|
| Email | | |
| Birthday | | Membership date: |
| Gender | | |
| Marital Status | | Wedding Anniversary: |

| Name | |
|---|---|
| Address | |
| | |

| Phone Numbers | Mobile: | Home: |
|---|---|---|
| Email | | |
| Birthday | | Membership date: |
| Gender | | |
| Marital Status | | Wedding Anniversary: |

| Name | |
|---|---|
| Address | |
| | |

| Phone Numbers | Mobile: | Home: |
|---|---|---|
| Email | | |
| Birthday | | Membership date: |
| Gender | | |
| Marital Status | | Wedding Anniversary: |

# L

| | |
|---|---|
| **Name** | |
| **Address** | |
| | |

| **Phone Numbers** | **Mobile:** | **Home:** |
|---|---|---|

| | | |
|---|---|---|
| **Email** | | |
| **Birthday** | | **Membership date:** |
| **Gender** | | |
| **Marital Status** | | **Wedding Anniversary:** |

| | |
|---|---|
| **Name** | |
| **Address** | |
| | |

| **Phone Numbers** | **Mobile:** | **Home:** |
|---|---|---|

| | | |
|---|---|---|
| **Email** | | |
| **Birthday** | | **Membership date:** |
| **Gender** | | |
| **Marital Status** | | **Wedding Anniversary:** |

| | |
|---|---|
| **Name** | |
| **Address** | |
| | |

| **Phone Numbers** | **Mobile:** | **Home:** |
|---|---|---|

| | | |
|---|---|---|
| **Email** | | |
| **Birthday** | | **Membership date:** |
| **Gender** | | |
| **Marital Status** | | **Wedding Anniversary:** |

## L

| Name | |
|---|---|
| Address | |
| | |
| Phone Numbers | Mobile:            Home: |
| Email | |
| Birthday |          Membership date: |
| Gender | |
| Marital Status |          Wedding Anniversary: |

| Name | |
|---|---|
| Address | |
| | |
| Phone Numbers | Mobile:            Home: |
| Email | |
| Birthday |          Membership date: |
| Gender | |
| Marital Status |          Wedding Anniversary: |

| Name | |
|---|---|
| Address | |
| | |
| Phone Numbers | Mobile:            Home: |
| Email | |
| Birthday |          Membership date: |
| Gender | |
| Marital Status |          Wedding Anniversary: |

# L

| Name | |
|---|---|
| Address | |
| | |
| **Phone Numbers** | **Mobile:**        **Home:** |
| Email | |
| Birthday | Membership date: |
| Gender | |
| Marital Status | Wedding Anniversary: |

| Name | |
|---|---|
| Address | |
| | |
| **Phone Numbers** | **Mobile:**        **Home:** |
| Email | |
| Birthday | Membership date: |
| Gender | |
| Marital Status | Wedding Anniversary: |

| Name | |
|---|---|
| Address | |
| | |
| **Phone Numbers** | **Mobile:**        **Home:** |
| Email | |
| Birthday | Membership date: |
| Gender | |
| Marital Status | Wedding Anniversary: |

## M

| Name | |
|---|---|
| Address | |
| | |
| Phone Numbers | Mobile: Home: |
| Email | |
| Birthday | Membership date: |
| Gender | |
| Marital Status | Wedding Anniversary: |

| Name | |
|---|---|
| Address | |
| | |
| Phone Numbers | Mobile: Home: |
| Email | |
| Birthday | Membership date: |
| Gender | |
| Marital Status | Wedding Anniversary: |

| Name | |
|---|---|
| Address | |
| | |
| Phone Numbers | Mobile: Home: |
| Email | |
| Birthday | Membership date: |
| Gender | |
| Marital Status | Wedding Anniversary: |

# M

| Name | |
|---|---|
| Address | |
| | |
| Phone Numbers | Mobile:        Home: |
| Email | |
| Birthday |       Membership date: |
| Gender | |
| Marital Status |       Wedding Anniversary: |

| Name | |
|---|---|
| Address | |
| | |
| Phone Numbers | Mobile:        Home: |
| Email | |
| Birthday |       Membership date: |
| Gender | |
| Marital Status |       Wedding Anniversary: |

| Name | |
|---|---|
| Address | |
| | |
| Phone Numbers | Mobile:        Home: |
| Email | |
| Birthday |       Membership date: |
| Gender | |
| Marital Status |       Wedding Anniversary: |

## M

| Name | |
|---|---|
| Address | |
| | |

| Phone Numbers | Mobile: | | Home: |
|---|---|---|---|
| Email | | | |
| Birthday | | Membership date: | |
| Gender | | | |
| Marital Status | | Wedding Anniversary: | |

| Name | |
|---|---|
| Address | |
| | |

| Phone Numbers | Mobile: | | Home: |
|---|---|---|---|
| Email | | | |
| Birthday | | Membership date: | |
| Gender | | | |
| Marital Status | | Wedding Anniversary: | |

| Name | |
|---|---|
| Address | |
| | |

| Phone Numbers | Mobile: | | Home: |
|---|---|---|---|
| Email | | | |
| Birthday | | Membership date: | |
| Gender | | | |
| Marital Status | | Wedding Anniversary: | |

## M

| Name | |
|---|---|
| Address | |
| | |
| Phone Numbers | Mobile: | Home: |
| Email | |
| Birthday | Membership date: |
| Gender | |
| Marital Status | Wedding Anniversary: |

| Name | |
|---|---|
| Address | |
| | |
| Phone Numbers | Mobile: | Home: |
| Email | |
| Birthday | Membership date: |
| Gender | |
| Marital Status | Wedding Anniversary: |

| Name | |
|---|---|
| Address | |
| | |
| Phone Numbers | Mobile: | Home: |
| Email | |
| Birthday | Membership date: |
| Gender | |
| Marital Status | Wedding Anniversary: |

# N

| Name | |
|---|---|
| Address | |
| | |

| Phone Numbers | Mobile: | Home: |
|---|---|---|

| Email | |
|---|---|

| Birthday | | Membership date: |
|---|---|---|

| Gender | |
|---|---|

| Marital Status | | Wedding Anniversary: |
|---|---|---|

| Name | |
|---|---|
| Address | |
| | |

| Phone Numbers | Mobile: | Home: |
|---|---|---|

| Email | |
|---|---|

| Birthday | | Membership date: |
|---|---|---|

| Gender | |
|---|---|

| Marital Status | | Wedding Anniversary: |
|---|---|---|

| Name | |
|---|---|
| Address | |
| | |

| Phone Numbers | Mobile: | Home: |
|---|---|---|

| Email | |
|---|---|

| Birthday | | Membership date: |
|---|---|---|

| Gender | |
|---|---|

| Marital Status | | Wedding Anniversary: |
|---|---|---|

# N

| Name | |
|---|---|
| Address | |
| | |
| Phone Numbers | Mobile: | Home: |
| Email | |
| Birthday | Membership date: |
| Gender | |
| Marital Status | Wedding Anniversary: |

| Name | |
|---|---|
| Address | |
| | |
| Phone Numbers | Mobile: | Home: |
| Email | |
| Birthday | Membership date: |
| Gender | |
| Marital Status | Wedding Anniversary: |

| Name | |
|---|---|
| Address | |
| | |
| Phone Numbers | Mobile: | Home: |
| Email | |
| Birthday | Membership date: |
| Gender | |
| Marital Status | Wedding Anniversary: |

# N

| Name | |
|---|---|
| Address | |
| | |

| Phone Numbers | Mobile: | Home: |
|---|---|---|

| Email | |
|---|---|

| Birthday | | Membership date: |
|---|---|---|

| Gender | |
|---|---|

| Marital Status | | Wedding Anniversary: |
|---|---|---|

| Name | |
|---|---|
| Address | |
| | |

| Phone Numbers | Mobile: | Home: |
|---|---|---|

| Email | |
|---|---|

| Birthday | | Membership date: |
|---|---|---|

| Gender | |
|---|---|

| Marital Status | | Wedding Anniversary: |
|---|---|---|

| Name | |
|---|---|
| Address | |
| | |

| Phone Numbers | Mobile: | Home: |
|---|---|---|

| Email | |
|---|---|

| Birthday | | Membership date: |
|---|---|---|

| Gender | |
|---|---|

| Marital Status | | Wedding Anniversary: |
|---|---|---|

## N

| Name | |
|---|---|
| Address | |
| | |

| Phone Numbers | Mobile: | Home: |
|---|---|---|
| Email | | |
| Birthday | | Membership date: |
| Gender | | |
| Marital Status | | Wedding Anniversary: |

| Name | |
|---|---|
| Address | |
| | |

| Phone Numbers | Mobile: | Home: |
|---|---|---|
| Email | | |
| Birthday | | Membership date: |
| Gender | | |
| Marital Status | | Wedding Anniversary: |

| Name | |
|---|---|
| Address | |
| | |

| Phone Numbers | Mobile: | Home: |
|---|---|---|
| Email | | |
| Birthday | | Membership date: |
| Gender | | |
| Marital Status | | Wedding Anniversary: |

# O

| Name | |
|---|---|
| Address | |
| | |

| Phone Numbers | Mobile: | Home: |
|---|---|---|

| Email | |
|---|---|

| Birthday | Membership date: |
|---|---|

| Gender | |
|---|---|

| Marital Status | Wedding Anniversary: |
|---|---|

| Name | |
|---|---|
| Address | |
| | |

| Phone Numbers | Mobile: | Home: |
|---|---|---|

| Email | |
|---|---|

| Birthday | Membership date: |
|---|---|

| Gender | |
|---|---|

| Marital Status | Wedding Anniversary: |
|---|---|

| Name | |
|---|---|
| Address | |
| | |

| Phone Numbers | Mobile: | Home: |
|---|---|---|

| Email | |
|---|---|

| Birthday | Membership date: |
|---|---|

| Gender | |
|---|---|

| Marital Status | Wedding Anniversary: |
|---|---|

## O

| Name | |
|---|---|
| Address | |
| | |

| Phone Numbers | Mobile: | Home: |
|---|---|---|

| Email | |
|---|---|

| Birthday | | Membership date: |
|---|---|---|

| Gender | |
|---|---|

| Marital Status | Wedding Anniversary: |
|---|---|

| Name | |
|---|---|
| Address | |
| | |

| Phone Numbers | Mobile: | Home: |
|---|---|---|

| Email | |
|---|---|

| Birthday | | Membership date: |
|---|---|---|

| Gender | |
|---|---|

| Marital Status | Wedding Anniversary: |
|---|---|

| Name | |
|---|---|
| Address | |
| | |

| Phone Numbers | Mobile: | Home: |
|---|---|---|

| Email | |
|---|---|

| Birthday | | Membership date: |
|---|---|---|

| Gender | |
|---|---|

| Marital Status | Wedding Anniversary: |
|---|---|

# O

| Name | |
|---|---|
| Address | |
| | |

| Phone Numbers | Mobile: | Home: |
|---|---|---|

| Email | |
|---|---|

| Birthday | | Membership date: |
|---|---|---|

| Gender | |
|---|---|

| Marital Status | | Wedding Anniversary: |
|---|---|---|

| Name | |
|---|---|
| Address | |
| | |

| Phone Numbers | Mobile: | Home: |
|---|---|---|

| Email | |
|---|---|

| Birthday | | Membership date: |
|---|---|---|

| Gender | |
|---|---|

| Marital Status | | Wedding Anniversary: |
|---|---|---|

| Name | |
|---|---|
| Address | |
| | |

| Phone Numbers | Mobile: | Home: |
|---|---|---|

| Email | |
|---|---|

| Birthday | | Membership date: |
|---|---|---|

| Gender | |
|---|---|

| Marital Status | | Wedding Anniversary: |
|---|---|---|

# O

| Name | |
|---|---|
| Address | |
| | |

| Phone Numbers | Mobile: | Home: |
|---|---|---|
| Email | | |
| Birthday | | Membership date: |
| Gender | | |
| Marital Status | | Wedding Anniversary: |

| Name | |
|---|---|
| Address | |
| | |

| Phone Numbers | Mobile: | Home: |
|---|---|---|
| Email | | |
| Birthday | | Membership date: |
| Gender | | |
| Marital Status | | Wedding Anniversary: |

| Name | |
|---|---|
| Address | |
| | |

| Phone Numbers | Mobile: | Home: |
|---|---|---|
| Email | | |
| Birthday | | Membership date: |
| Gender | | |
| Marital Status | | Wedding Anniversary: |

# P

| Name | |
|---|---|
| Address | |
| | |

| Phone Numbers | Mobile: | Home: |
|---|---|---|

| Email | |
|---|---|

| Birthday | | Membership date: |
|---|---|---|

| Gender | |
|---|---|

| Marital Status | | Wedding Anniversary: |
|---|---|---|

| Name | |
|---|---|
| Address | |
| | |

| Phone Numbers | Mobile: | Home: |
|---|---|---|

| Email | |
|---|---|

| Birthday | | Membership date: |
|---|---|---|

| Gender | |
|---|---|

| Marital Status | | Wedding Anniversary: |
|---|---|---|

| Name | |
|---|---|
| Address | |
| | |

| Phone Numbers | Mobile: | Home: |
|---|---|---|

| Email | |
|---|---|

| Birthday | | Membership date: |
|---|---|---|

| Gender | |
|---|---|

| Marital Status | | Wedding Anniversary: |
|---|---|---|

## P

| Name | |
|---|---|
| Address | |
| | |

| Phone Numbers | Mobile: | Home: |
|---|---|---|

| Email | |
|---|---|

| Birthday | Membership date: |
|---|---|

| Gender | |
|---|---|

| Marital Status | Wedding Anniversary: |
|---|---|

| Name | |
|---|---|
| Address | |
| | |

| Phone Numbers | Mobile: | Home: |
|---|---|---|

| Email | |
|---|---|

| Birthday | Membership date: |
|---|---|

| Gender | |
|---|---|

| Marital Status | Wedding Anniversary: |
|---|---|

| Name | |
|---|---|
| Address | |
| | |

| Phone Numbers | Mobile: | Home: |
|---|---|---|

| Email | |
|---|---|

| Birthday | Membership date: |
|---|---|

| Gender | |
|---|---|

| Marital Status | Wedding Anniversary: |
|---|---|

# P

| Name | |
|---|---|
| Address | |
| | |
| Phone Numbers | Mobile: Home: |
| Email | |
| Birthday | Membership date: |
| Gender | |
| Marital Status | Wedding Anniversary: |

| Name | |
|---|---|
| Address | |
| | |
| Phone Numbers | Mobile: Home: |
| Email | |
| Birthday | Membership date: |
| Gender | |
| Marital Status | Wedding Anniversary: |

| Name | |
|---|---|
| Address | |
| | |
| Phone Numbers | Mobile: Home: |
| Email | |
| Birthday | Membership date: |
| Gender | |
| Marital Status | Wedding Anniversary: |

**P**

| Name | |
|---|---|
| Address | |
| | |

| Phone Numbers | Mobile: | Home: |
|---|---|---|

| Email | |
|---|---|

| Birthday | | Membership date: |
|---|---|---|

| Gender | |
|---|---|

| Marital Status | | Wedding Anniversary: |
|---|---|---|

| Name | |
|---|---|
| Address | |
| | |

| Phone Numbers | Mobile: | Home: |
|---|---|---|

| Email | |
|---|---|

| Birthday | | Membership date: |
|---|---|---|

| Gender | |
|---|---|

| Marital Status | | Wedding Anniversary: |
|---|---|---|

| Name | |
|---|---|
| Address | |
| | |

| Phone Numbers | Mobile: | Home: |
|---|---|---|

| Email | |
|---|---|

| Birthday | | Membership date: |
|---|---|---|

| Gender | |
|---|---|

| Marital Status | | Wedding Anniversary: |
|---|---|---|

# Q

| Name | |
|---|---|
| Address | |
| | |
| Phone Numbers | Mobile: | Home: |
| Email | |
| Birthday | | Membership date: |
| Gender | |
| Marital Status | | Wedding Anniversary: |

| Name | |
|---|---|
| Address | |
| | |
| Phone Numbers | Mobile: | Home: |
| Email | |
| Birthday | | Membership date: |
| Gender | |
| Marital Status | | Wedding Anniversary: |

| Name | |
|---|---|
| Address | |
| | |
| Phone Numbers | Mobile: | Home: |
| Email | |
| Birthday | | Membership date: |
| Gender | |
| Marital Status | | Wedding Anniversary: |

# Q

| Name | |
|---|---|
| Address | |
| | |

| Phone Numbers | Mobile: | Home: |
|---|---|---|
| Email | | |
| Birthday | | Membership date: |
| Gender | | |
| Marital Status | | Wedding Anniversary: |

| Name | |
|---|---|
| Address | |
| | |

| Phone Numbers | Mobile: | Home: |
|---|---|---|
| Email | | |
| Birthday | | Membership date: |
| Gender | | |
| Marital Status | | Wedding Anniversary: |

| Name | |
|---|---|
| Address | |
| | |

| Phone Numbers | Mobile: | Home: |
|---|---|---|
| Email | | |
| Birthday | | Membership date: |
| Gender | | |
| Marital Status | | Wedding Anniversary: |

# Q

| Name | |
|---|---|
| Address | |
| | |

| Phone Numbers | Mobile: | Home: |
|---|---|---|

| Email | |
|---|---|

| Birthday | | Membership date: |
|---|---|---|

| Gender | |
|---|---|

| Marital Status | | Wedding Anniversary: |
|---|---|---|

| Name | |
|---|---|
| Address | |
| | |

| Phone Numbers | Mobile: | Home: |
|---|---|---|

| Email | |
|---|---|

| Birthday | | Membership date: |
|---|---|---|

| Gender | |
|---|---|

| Marital Status | | Wedding Anniversary: |
|---|---|---|

| Name | |
|---|---|
| Address | |
| | |

| Phone Numbers | Mobile: | Home: |
|---|---|---|

| Email | |
|---|---|

| Birthday | | Membership date: |
|---|---|---|

| Gender | |
|---|---|

| Marital Status | | Wedding Anniversary: |
|---|---|---|

# Q

| Name | |
|---|---|
| Address | |
| | |
| Phone Numbers | Mobile: | Home: |
| Email | |
| Birthday | Membership date: |
| Gender | |
| Marital Status | Wedding Anniversary: |

| Name | |
|---|---|
| Address | |
| | |
| Phone Numbers | Mobile: | Home: |
| Email | |
| Birthday | Membership date: |
| Gender | |
| Marital Status | Wedding Anniversary: |

| Name | |
|---|---|
| Address | |
| | |
| Phone Numbers | Mobile: | Home: |
| Email | |
| Birthday | Membership date: |
| Gender | |
| Marital Status | Wedding Anniversary: |

# R

| | |
|---|---|
| **Name** | |
| **Address** | |
| | |
| **Phone Numbers** | Mobile:        Home: |
| **Email** | |
| **Birthday** |       Membership date: |
| **Gender** | |
| **Marital Status** |     Wedding Anniversary: |

| | |
|---|---|
| **Name** | |
| **Address** | |
| | |
| **Phone Numbers** | Mobile:        Home: |
| **Email** | |
| **Birthday** |       Membership date: |
| **Gender** | |
| **Marital Status** |     Wedding Anniversary: |

| | |
|---|---|
| **Name** | |
| **Address** | |
| | |
| **Phone Numbers** | Mobile:        Home: |
| **Email** | |
| **Birthday** |       Membership date: |
| **Gender** | |
| **Marital Status** |     Wedding Anniversary: |

## R

| Name | |
|---|---|
| Address | |
| | |

| Phone Numbers | Mobile: | Home: |
|---|---|---|
| Email | | |
| Birthday | | Membership date: |
| Gender | | |
| Marital Status | | Wedding Anniversary: |

| Name | |
|---|---|
| Address | |
| | |

| Phone Numbers | Mobile: | Home: |
|---|---|---|
| Email | | |
| Birthday | | Membership date: |
| Gender | | |
| Marital Status | | Wedding Anniversary: |

| Name | |
|---|---|
| Address | |
| | |

| Phone Numbers | Mobile: | Home: |
|---|---|---|
| Email | | |
| Birthday | | Membership date: |
| Gender | | |
| Marital Status | | Wedding Anniversary: |

# R

| Name | |
|---|---|
| Address | |
| | |
| Phone Numbers | Mobile: | Home: |
| Email | |
| Birthday | | Membership date: |
| Gender | |
| Marital Status | | Wedding Anniversary: |

| Name | |
|---|---|
| Address | |
| | |
| Phone Numbers | Mobile: | Home: |
| Email | |
| Birthday | | Membership date: |
| Gender | |
| Marital Status | | Wedding Anniversary: |

| Name | |
|---|---|
| Address | |
| | |
| Phone Numbers | Mobile: | Home: |
| Email | |
| Birthday | | Membership date: |
| Gender | |
| Marital Status | | Wedding Anniversary: |

# R

| Name | |
|---|---|
| Address | |
| | |
| Phone Numbers | Mobile:         Home: |
| Email | |
| Birthday |        Membership date: |
| Gender | |
| Marital Status |        Wedding Anniversary: |

| Name | |
|---|---|
| Address | |
| | |
| Phone Numbers | Mobile:         Home: |
| Email | |
| Birthday |        Membership date: |
| Gender | |
| Marital Status |        Wedding Anniversary: |

| Name | |
|---|---|
| Address | |
| | |
| Phone Numbers | Mobile:         Home: |
| Email | |
| Birthday |        Membership date: |
| Gender | |
| Marital Status |        Wedding Anniversary: |

## S

| Name | |
|---|---|
| Address | |
| | |
| Phone Numbers | Mobile: | Home: |
| Email | |
| Birthday | Membership date: |
| Gender | |
| Marital Status | Wedding Anniversary: |

| Name | |
|---|---|
| Address | |
| | |
| Phone Numbers | Mobile: | Home: |
| Email | |
| Birthday | Membership date: |
| Gender | |
| Marital Status | Wedding Anniversary: |

| Name | |
|---|---|
| Address | |
| | |
| Phone Numbers | Mobile: | Home: |
| Email | |
| Birthday | Membership date: |
| Gender | |
| Marital Status | Wedding Anniversary: |

## S

| Name | |
|------|---|
| Address | |
| | |

| Phone Numbers | Mobile: | Home: |
|---------------|---------|-------|
| Email | | |
| Birthday | | Membership date: |
| Gender | | |
| Marital Status | | Wedding Anniversary: |

| Name | |
|------|---|
| Address | |
| | |

| Phone Numbers | Mobile: | Home: |
|---------------|---------|-------|
| Email | | |
| Birthday | | Membership date: |
| Gender | | |
| Marital Status | | Wedding Anniversary: |

| Name | |
|------|---|
| Address | |
| | |

| Phone Numbers | Mobile: | Home: |
|---------------|---------|-------|
| Email | | |
| Birthday | | Membership date: |
| Gender | | |
| Marital Status | | Wedding Anniversary: |

# S

| Name | |
|---|---|
| Address | |
| | |

| Phone Numbers | Mobile: | Home: |
|---|---|---|

| Email | |
|---|---|

| Birthday | | Membership date: |
|---|---|---|

| Gender | |
|---|---|

| Marital Status | | Wedding Anniversary: |
|---|---|---|

| Name | |
|---|---|
| Address | |
| | |

| Phone Numbers | Mobile: | Home: |
|---|---|---|

| Email | |
|---|---|

| Birthday | | Membership date: |
|---|---|---|

| Gender | |
|---|---|

| Marital Status | | Wedding Anniversary: |
|---|---|---|

| Name | |
|---|---|
| Address | |
| | |

| Phone Numbers | Mobile: | Home: |
|---|---|---|

| Email | |
|---|---|

| Birthday | | Membership date: |
|---|---|---|

| Gender | |
|---|---|

| Marital Status | | Wedding Anniversary: |
|---|---|---|

## S

| Name | |
|---|---|
| Address | |
| | |

| Phone Numbers | Mobile: | Home: |
|---|---|---|
| Email | | |
| Birthday | | Membership date: |
| Gender | | |
| Marital Status | | Wedding Anniversary: |

| Name | |
|---|---|
| Address | |
| | |

| Phone Numbers | Mobile: | Home: |
|---|---|---|
| Email | | |
| Birthday | | Membership date: |
| Gender | | |
| Marital Status | | Wedding Anniversary: |

| Name | |
|---|---|
| Address | |
| | |

| Phone Numbers | Mobile: | Home: |
|---|---|---|
| Email | | |
| Birthday | | Membership date: |
| Gender | | |
| Marital Status | | Wedding Anniversary: |

## T

| Name | |
|---|---|
| Address | |
| | |

| Phone Numbers | Mobile: | Home: |
|---|---|---|

| Email | |
|---|---|

| Birthday | | Membership date: |
|---|---|---|

| Gender | |
|---|---|

| Marital Status | | Wedding Anniversary: |
|---|---|---|

| Name | |
|---|---|
| Address | |
| | |

| Phone Numbers | Mobile: | Home: |
|---|---|---|

| Email | |
|---|---|

| Birthday | | Membership date: |
|---|---|---|

| Gender | |
|---|---|

| Marital Status | | Wedding Anniversary: |
|---|---|---|

| Name | |
|---|---|
| Address | |
| | |

| Phone Numbers | Mobile: | Home: |
|---|---|---|

| Email | |
|---|---|

| Birthday | | Membership date: |
|---|---|---|

| Gender | |
|---|---|

| Marital Status | | Wedding Anniversary: |
|---|---|---|

# T

| Name | |
|---|---|
| Address | |
| | |
| Phone Numbers | Mobile: | Home: |
| Email | |
| Birthday | Membership date: |
| Gender | |
| Marital Status | Wedding Anniversary: |

| Name | |
|---|---|
| Address | |
| | |
| Phone Numbers | Mobile: | Home: |
| Email | |
| Birthday | Membership date: |
| Gender | |
| Marital Status | Wedding Anniversary: |

| Name | |
|---|---|
| Address | |
| | |
| Phone Numbers | Mobile: | Home: |
| Email | |
| Birthday | Membership date: |
| Gender | |
| Marital Status | Wedding Anniversary: |

# T

| Name | |
|---|---|
| Address | |
| | |

| Phone Numbers | Mobile: | Home: |
|---|---|---|

| Email | |
|---|---|

| Birthday | | Membership date: |
|---|---|---|

| Gender | |
|---|---|

| Marital Status | | Wedding Anniversary: |
|---|---|---|

| Name | |
|---|---|
| Address | |
| | |

| Phone Numbers | Mobile: | Home: |
|---|---|---|

| Email | |
|---|---|

| Birthday | | Membership date: |
|---|---|---|

| Gender | |
|---|---|

| Marital Status | | Wedding Anniversary: |
|---|---|---|

| Name | |
|---|---|
| Address | |
| | |

| Phone Numbers | Mobile: | Home: |
|---|---|---|

| Email | |
|---|---|

| Birthday | | Membership date: |
|---|---|---|

| Gender | |
|---|---|

| Marital Status | | Wedding Anniversary: |
|---|---|---|

# T

| Name | |
|---|---|
| Address | |
| | |

| Phone Numbers | Mobile: | Home: |
|---|---|---|
| Email | | |
| Birthday | | Membership date: |
| Gender | | |
| Marital Status | | Wedding Anniversary: |

| Name | |
|---|---|
| Address | |
| | |

| Phone Numbers | Mobile: | Home: |
|---|---|---|
| Email | | |
| Birthday | | Membership date: |
| Gender | | |
| Marital Status | | Wedding Anniversary: |

| Name | |
|---|---|
| Address | |
| | |

| Phone Numbers | Mobile: | Home: |
|---|---|---|
| Email | | |
| Birthday | | Membership date: |
| Gender | | |
| Marital Status | | Wedding Anniversary: |

# U

| Name | |
|---|---|
| Address | |
| | |

| Phone Numbers | Mobile: | Home: |
|---|---|---|

| Email | |
|---|---|

| Birthday | | Membership date: |
|---|---|---|

| Gender | |
|---|---|

| Marital Status | | Wedding Anniversary: |
|---|---|---|

| Name | |
|---|---|
| Address | |
| | |

| Phone Numbers | Mobile: | Home: |
|---|---|---|

| Email | |
|---|---|

| Birthday | | Membership date: |
|---|---|---|

| Gender | |
|---|---|

| Marital Status | | Wedding Anniversary: |
|---|---|---|

| Name | |
|---|---|
| Address | |
| | |

| Phone Numbers | Mobile: | Home: |
|---|---|---|

| Email | |
|---|---|

| Birthday | | Membership date: |
|---|---|---|

| Gender | |
|---|---|

| Marital Status | | Wedding Anniversary: |
|---|---|---|

## U

| Name | |
|---|---|
| Address | |
| | |

| Phone Numbers | Mobile: | Home: |
|---|---|---|
| Email | | |
| Birthday | | Membership date: |
| Gender | | |
| Marital Status | | Wedding Anniversary: |

| Name | |
|---|---|
| Address | |
| | |

| Phone Numbers | Mobile: | Home: |
|---|---|---|
| Email | | |
| Birthday | | Membership date: |
| Gender | | |
| Marital Status | | Wedding Anniversary: |

| Name | |
|---|---|
| Address | |
| | |

| Phone Numbers | Mobile: | Home: |
|---|---|---|
| Email | | |
| Birthday | | Membership date: |
| Gender | | |
| Marital Status | | Wedding Anniversary: |

## U

| Name | |
|---|---|
| Address | |
| | |

| Phone Numbers | Mobile: | Home: |
|---|---|---|

| Email | |
|---|---|

| Birthday | | Membership date: |
|---|---|---|

| Gender | |
|---|---|

| Marital Status | | Wedding Anniversary: |
|---|---|---|

| Name | |
|---|---|
| Address | |
| | |

| Phone Numbers | Mobile: | Home: |
|---|---|---|

| Email | |
|---|---|

| Birthday | | Membership date: |
|---|---|---|

| Gender | |
|---|---|

| Marital Status | | Wedding Anniversary: |
|---|---|---|

| Name | |
|---|---|
| Address | |
| | |

| Phone Numbers | Mobile: | Home: |
|---|---|---|

| Email | |
|---|---|

| Birthday | | Membership date: |
|---|---|---|

| Gender | |
|---|---|

| Marital Status | | Wedding Anniversary: |
|---|---|---|

# U

| Name | |
|---|---|
| Address | |
| | |

| Phone Numbers | Mobile: | Home: |
|---|---|---|
| Email | | |
| Birthday | | Membership date: |
| Gender | | |
| Marital Status | | Wedding Anniversary: |

| Name | |
|---|---|
| Address | |
| | |

| Phone Numbers | Mobile: | Home: |
|---|---|---|
| Email | | |
| Birthday | | Membership date: |
| Gender | | |
| Marital Status | | Wedding Anniversary: |

| Name | |
|---|---|
| Address | |
| | |

| Phone Numbers | Mobile: | Home: |
|---|---|---|
| Email | | |
| Birthday | | Membership date: |
| Gender | | |
| Marital Status | | Wedding Anniversary: |

# V

| Name | |
|---|---|
| Address | |
| | |

| Phone Numbers | Mobile: | Home: |
|---|---|---|

| Email | |
|---|---|

| Birthday | | Membership date: |
|---|---|---|

| Gender | |
|---|---|

| Marital Status | | Wedding Anniversary: |
|---|---|---|

| Name | |
|---|---|
| Address | |
| | |

| Phone Numbers | Mobile: | Home: |
|---|---|---|

| Email | |
|---|---|

| Birthday | | Membership date: |
|---|---|---|

| Gender | |
|---|---|

| Marital Status | | Wedding Anniversary: |
|---|---|---|

| Name | |
|---|---|
| Address | |
| | |

| Phone Numbers | Mobile: | Home: |
|---|---|---|

| Email | |
|---|---|

| Birthday | | Membership date: |
|---|---|---|

| Gender | |
|---|---|

| Marital Status | | Wedding Anniversary: |
|---|---|---|

# V

| Name | |
|---|---|
| Address | |
| | |

| Phone Numbers | Mobile: | Home: |
|---|---|---|
| Email | | |
| Birthday | | Membership date: |
| Gender | | |
| Marital Status | | Wedding Anniversary: |

| Name | |
|---|---|
| Address | |
| | |

| Phone Numbers | Mobile: | Home: |
|---|---|---|
| Email | | |
| Birthday | | Membership date: |
| Gender | | |
| Marital Status | | Wedding Anniversary: |

| Name | |
|---|---|
| Address | |
| | |

| Phone Numbers | Mobile: | Home: |
|---|---|---|
| Email | | |
| Birthday | | Membership date: |
| Gender | | |
| Marital Status | | Wedding Anniversary: |

## V

| Name | |
|---|---|
| Address | |
| | |

| Phone Numbers | Mobile: | Home: |
|---|---|---|

| Email | |
|---|---|

| Birthday | | Membership date: |
|---|---|---|

| Gender | |
|---|---|

| Marital Status | | Wedding Anniversary: |
|---|---|---|

| Name | |
|---|---|
| Address | |
| | |

| Phone Numbers | Mobile: | Home: |
|---|---|---|

| Email | |
|---|---|

| Birthday | | Membership date: |
|---|---|---|

| Gender | |
|---|---|

| Marital Status | | Wedding Anniversary: |
|---|---|---|

| Name | |
|---|---|
| Address | |
| | |

| Phone Numbers | Mobile: | Home: |
|---|---|---|

| Email | |
|---|---|

| Birthday | | Membership date: |
|---|---|---|

| Gender | |
|---|---|

| Marital Status | | Wedding Anniversary: |
|---|---|---|

# V

| Name | |
|---|---|
| Address | |
| | |

| Phone Numbers | Mobile: | Home: |
|---|---|---|
| Email | | |
| Birthday | | Membership date: |
| Gender | | |
| Marital Status | | Wedding Anniversary: |

| Name | |
|---|---|
| Address | |
| | |

| Phone Numbers | Mobile: | Home: |
|---|---|---|
| Email | | |
| Birthday | | Membership date: |
| Gender | | |
| Marital Status | | Wedding Anniversary: |

| Name | |
|---|---|
| Address | |
| | |

| Phone Numbers | Mobile: | Home: |
|---|---|---|
| Email | | |
| Birthday | | Membership date: |
| Gender | | |
| Marital Status | | Wedding Anniversary: |

# W

| Name | |
|---|---|
| Address | |
| | |

| Phone Numbers | Mobile: | Home: |
|---|---|---|

| Email | |
|---|---|

| Birthday | | Membership date: |
|---|---|---|

| Gender | |
|---|---|

| Marital Status | | Wedding Anniversary: |
|---|---|---|

| Name | |
|---|---|
| Address | |
| | |

| Phone Numbers | Mobile: | Home: |
|---|---|---|

| Email | |
|---|---|

| Birthday | | Membership date: |
|---|---|---|

| Gender | |
|---|---|

| Marital Status | | Wedding Anniversary: |
|---|---|---|

| Name | |
|---|---|
| Address | |
| | |

| Phone Numbers | Mobile: | Home: |
|---|---|---|

| Email | |
|---|---|

| Birthday | | Membership date: |
|---|---|---|

| Gender | |
|---|---|

| Marital Status | | Wedding Anniversary: |
|---|---|---|

# W

| Name | |
|---|---|
| Address | |
| | |

| Phone Numbers | Mobile: | Home: |
|---|---|---|
| Email | | |
| Birthday | | Membership date: |
| Gender | | |
| Marital Status | | Wedding Anniversary: |

| Name | |
|---|---|
| Address | |
| | |

| Phone Numbers | Mobile: | Home: |
|---|---|---|
| Email | | |
| Birthday | | Membership date: |
| Gender | | |
| Marital Status | | Wedding Anniversary: |

| Name | |
|---|---|
| Address | |
| | |

| Phone Numbers | Mobile: | Home: |
|---|---|---|
| Email | | |
| Birthday | | Membership date: |
| Gender | | |
| Marital Status | | Wedding Anniversary: |

# W

| Name | |
|---|---|
| Address | |
| | |
| Phone Numbers | Mobile: Home: |
| Email | |
| Birthday | Membership date: |
| Gender | |
| Marital Status | Wedding Anniversary: |

| Name | |
|---|---|
| Address | |
| | |
| Phone Numbers | Mobile: Home: |
| Email | |
| Birthday | Membership date: |
| Gender | |
| Marital Status | Wedding Anniversary: |

| Name | |
|---|---|
| Address | |
| | |
| Phone Numbers | Mobile: Home: |
| Email | |
| Birthday | Membership date: |
| Gender | |
| Marital Status | Wedding Anniversary: |

## W

| Name | |
|---|---|
| Address | |
| | |
| Phone Numbers | Mobile: | Home: |
| Email | |
| Birthday | | Membership date: |
| Gender | |
| Marital Status | | Wedding Anniversary: |

| Name | |
|---|---|
| Address | |
| | |
| Phone Numbers | Mobile: | Home: |
| Email | |
| Birthday | | Membership date: |
| Gender | |
| Marital Status | | Wedding Anniversary: |

| Name | |
|---|---|
| Address | |
| | |
| Phone Numbers | Mobile: | Home: |
| Email | |
| Birthday | | Membership date: |
| Gender | |
| Marital Status | | Wedding Anniversary: |

## X

| Name | |
|---|---|
| Address | |
| | |
| Phone Numbers | Mobile: | Home: |
| Email | |
| Birthday | Membership date: |
| Gender | |
| Marital Status | Wedding Anniversary: |

| Name | |
|---|---|
| Address | |
| | |
| Phone Numbers | Mobile: | Home: |
| Email | |
| Birthday | Membership date: |
| Gender | |
| Marital Status | Wedding Anniversary: |

| Name | |
|---|---|
| Address | |
| | |
| Phone Numbers | Mobile: | Home: |
| Email | |
| Birthday | Membership date: |
| Gender | |
| Marital Status | Wedding Anniversary: |

# X

| Name | |
|---|---|
| Address | |
| | |
| Phone Numbers | Mobile: Home: |
| Email | |
| Birthday | Membership date: |
| Gender | |
| Marital Status | Wedding Anniversary: |

| Name | |
|---|---|
| Address | |
| | |
| Phone Numbers | Mobile: Home: |
| Email | |
| Birthday | Membership date: |
| Gender | |
| Marital Status | Wedding Anniversary: |

| Name | |
|---|---|
| Address | |
| | |
| Phone Numbers | Mobile: Home: |
| Email | |
| Birthday | Membership date: |
| Gender | |
| Marital Status | Wedding Anniversary: |

# X

| Name | |
|---|---|
| Address | |
| | |

| Phone Numbers | Mobile: | Home: |
|---|---|---|

| Email | |
|---|---|

| Birthday | | Membership date: |
|---|---|---|

| Gender | |
|---|---|

| Marital Status | | Wedding Anniversary: |
|---|---|---|

| Name | |
|---|---|
| Address | |
| | |

| Phone Numbers | Mobile: | Home: |
|---|---|---|

| Email | |
|---|---|

| Birthday | | Membership date: |
|---|---|---|

| Gender | |
|---|---|

| Marital Status | | Wedding Anniversary: |
|---|---|---|

| Name | |
|---|---|
| Address | |
| | |

| Phone Numbers | Mobile: | Home: |
|---|---|---|

| Email | |
|---|---|

| Birthday | | Membership date: |
|---|---|---|

| Gender | |
|---|---|

| Marital Status | | Wedding Anniversary: |
|---|---|---|

## X

| Name | |
|---|---|
| Address | |
| | |

| Phone Numbers | Mobile: | Home: |
|---|---|---|
| Email | | |
| Birthday | | Membership date: |
| Gender | | |
| Marital Status | | Wedding Anniversary: |

| Name | |
|---|---|
| Address | |
| | |

| Phone Numbers | Mobile: | Home: |
|---|---|---|
| Email | | |
| Birthday | | Membership date: |
| Gender | | |
| Marital Status | | Wedding Anniversary: |

| Name | |
|---|---|
| Address | |
| | |

| Phone Numbers | Mobile: | Home: |
|---|---|---|
| Email | | |
| Birthday | | Membership date: |
| Gender | | |
| Marital Status | | Wedding Anniversary: |

# Y

| Name | |
|---|---|
| Address | |
| | |

| Phone Numbers | Mobile: | Home: |
|---|---|---|

| Email | |
|---|---|

| Birthday | | Membership date: |
|---|---|---|

| Gender | |
|---|---|

| Marital Status | | Wedding Anniversary: |
|---|---|---|

| Name | |
|---|---|
| Address | |
| | |

| Phone Numbers | Mobile: | Home: |
|---|---|---|

| Email | |
|---|---|

| Birthday | | Membership date: |
|---|---|---|

| Gender | |
|---|---|

| Marital Status | | Wedding Anniversary: |
|---|---|---|

| Name | |
|---|---|
| Address | |
| | |

| Phone Numbers | Mobile: | Home: |
|---|---|---|

| Email | |
|---|---|

| Birthday | | Membership date: |
|---|---|---|

| Gender | |
|---|---|

| Marital Status | | Wedding Anniversary: |
|---|---|---|

## Y

| Name | |
|---|---|
| Address | |
| | |

| Phone Numbers | Mobile: | Home: |
|---|---|---|
| Email | | |
| Birthday | | Membership date: |
| Gender | | |
| Marital Status | | Wedding Anniversary: |

| Name | |
|---|---|
| Address | |
| | |

| Phone Numbers | Mobile: | Home: |
|---|---|---|
| Email | | |
| Birthday | | Membership date: |
| Gender | | |
| Marital Status | | Wedding Anniversary: |

| Name | |
|---|---|
| Address | |
| | |

| Phone Numbers | Mobile: | Home: |
|---|---|---|
| Email | | |
| Birthday | | Membership date: |
| Gender | | |
| Marital Status | | Wedding Anniversary: |

## Y

| Name | |
|---|---|
| Address | |
| | |
| Phone Numbers | Mobile: | Home: |
| Email | |
| Birthday | | Membership date: |
| Gender | |
| Marital Status | | Wedding Anniversary: |

| Name | |
|---|---|
| Address | |
| | |
| Phone Numbers | Mobile: | Home: |
| Email | |
| Birthday | | Membership date: |
| Gender | |
| Marital Status | | Wedding Anniversary: |

| Name | |
|---|---|
| Address | |
| | |
| Phone Numbers | Mobile: | Home: |
| Email | |
| Birthday | | Membership date: |
| Gender | |
| Marital Status | | Wedding Anniversary: |

# Y

| Name | |
|---|---|
| Address | |
| | |

| Phone Numbers | Mobile: | Home: |
|---|---|---|
| Email | | |
| Birthday | | Membership date: |
| Gender | | |
| Marital Status | | Wedding Anniversary: |

| Name | |
|---|---|
| Address | |
| | |

| Phone Numbers | Mobile: | Home: |
|---|---|---|
| Email | | |
| Birthday | | Membership date: |
| Gender | | |
| Marital Status | | Wedding Anniversary: |

| Name | |
|---|---|
| Address | |
| | |

| Phone Numbers | Mobile: | Home: |
|---|---|---|
| Email | | |
| Birthday | | Membership date: |
| Gender | | |
| Marital Status | | Wedding Anniversary: |

## Z

| Name | |
|---|---|
| Address | |
| | |

| Phone Numbers | Mobile: | Home: |
|---|---|---|
| Email | | |
| Birthday | | Membership date: |
| Gender | | |

| Marital Status | | Wedding Anniversary: |
|---|---|---|

| Name | |
|---|---|
| Address | |
| | |

| Phone Numbers | Mobile: | Home: |
|---|---|---|
| Email | | |
| Birthday | | Membership date: |
| Gender | | |

| Marital Status | | Wedding Anniversary: |
|---|---|---|

| Name | |
|---|---|
| Address | |
| | |

| Phone Numbers | Mobile: | Home: |
|---|---|---|
| Email | | |
| Birthday | | Membership date: |
| Gender | | |

| Marital Status | | Wedding Anniversary: |
|---|---|---|

# Z

| Name | |
|---|---|
| Address | |
| | |

| Phone Numbers | Mobile: | Home: |
|---|---|---|

| Email | |
|---|---|

| Birthday | | Membership date: |
|---|---|---|

| Gender | |
|---|---|

| Marital Status | | Wedding Anniversary: |
|---|---|---|

| Name | |
|---|---|
| Address | |
| | |

| Phone Numbers | Mobile: | Home: |
|---|---|---|

| Email | |
|---|---|

| Birthday | | Membership date: |
|---|---|---|

| Gender | |
|---|---|

| Marital Status | | Wedding Anniversary: |
|---|---|---|

| Name | |
|---|---|
| Address | |
| | |

| Phone Numbers | Mobile: | Home: |
|---|---|---|

| Email | |
|---|---|

| Birthday | | Membership date: |
|---|---|---|

| Gender | |
|---|---|

| Marital Status | | Wedding Anniversary: |
|---|---|---|

# Z

| Name | |
|---|---|
| Address | |
| | |

| Phone Numbers | Mobile: | Home: |
|---|---|---|

| Email | |
|---|---|

| Birthday | | Membership date: |
|---|---|---|

| Gender | |
|---|---|

| Marital Status | | Wedding Anniversary: |
|---|---|---|

| Name | |
|---|---|
| Address | |
| | |

| Phone Numbers | Mobile: | Home: |
|---|---|---|

| Email | |
|---|---|

| Birthday | | Membership date: |
|---|---|---|

| Gender | |
|---|---|

| Marital Status | | Wedding Anniversary: |
|---|---|---|

| Name | |
|---|---|
| Address | |
| | |

| Phone Numbers | Mobile: | Home: |
|---|---|---|

| Email | |
|---|---|

| Birthday | | Membership date: |
|---|---|---|

| Gender | |
|---|---|

| Marital Status | | Wedding Anniversary: |
|---|---|---|

## Z

| Name | |
|---|---|
| Address | |
| | |

| Phone Numbers | Mobile: | Home: |
|---|---|---|

| Email | |
|---|---|

| Birthday | Membership date: |
|---|---|

| Gender | |
|---|---|

| Marital Status | Wedding Anniversary: |
|---|---|

| Name | |
|---|---|
| Address | |
| | |

| Phone Numbers | Mobile: | Home: |
|---|---|---|

| Email | |
|---|---|

| Birthday | Membership date: |
|---|---|

| Gender | |
|---|---|

| Marital Status | Wedding Anniversary: |
|---|---|

| Name | |
|---|---|
| Address | |
| | |

| Phone Numbers | Mobile: | Home: |
|---|---|---|

| Email | |
|---|---|

| Birthday | Membership date: |
|---|---|

| Gender | |
|---|---|

| Marital Status | Wedding Anniversary: |
|---|---|

# NOTES

NOTES

# NOTES

# NOTES

# NOTES

NOTES

# NOTES

# NOTES

Made in the USA
Coppell, TX
27 July 2022

80512498R10070